The Twenty-First Century

WINNERS OF THE AMERICAN POETRY REVIEW/

HONICKMAN FIRST BOOK PRIZE

1998	Joshua Beckman, *Things Are Happening*
1999	Dana Levin, *In the Surgical Theatre*
2000	Anne Marie Macari, *Ivory Cradle*
2001	Ed Pavlic, *Paraph of Bone & Other Kinds of Blue*
2002	Kathleen Ossip, *The Search Engine*
2003	James McCorkle, *Evidences*
2004	Kevin Ducey, *Rhinoceros*
2005	Geoff Bouvier, *Living Room*
2006	David Roderick, *Blue Colonial*
2007	Gregory Pardlo, *Totem*
2008	Matthew Dickman, *All-American Poem*
2009	Laura McKee, *Uttermost Paradise Place*
2010	Melissa Stein, *Rough Honey*
2011	Nathaniel Perry, *Nine Acres*
2012	Tomás Q. Morín, *A Larger Country*
2013	Maria Hummel, *House & Fire*
2014	Katherine Bode-Lang, *The Reformation*
2015	Alicia Jo Rabins, *Divinity School*
2016	Heather Tone, *Likenesses*
2017	Tyree Daye, *River Hymns*
2018	Jacob Saenz, *Throwing the Crown*
2019	Taneum Bambrick, *Vantage*
2020	Chessy Normile, *Great Exodus, Great Wall, Great Party*
2021	Natasha Rao, *Latitude*
2022	Chelsea Harlan, *Bright Shade*
2023	Jane Huffman, *Public Abstract*

The Twenty-First Century

Jacob Eigen

The American Poetry Review
Philadelphia

 Direct all inquiries to: The American Poetry Review, 1906 Rittenhouse Square, Philadelphia, PA19103.

Cover art: Under the 7, Long Island City NYC, Justin Kim, 2017.
Book design and composition: Gopa & Ted2, Inc.
Distribution by Copper Canyon Press/Consortium

Library of Congress Control Number: 2024933258

ISBN 978-0-9860938-7-6, hardcover
ISBN 979-8-9875852-2-1, paperback

9 8 7 6 5 4 3 2 FIRST EDITION

For my parents
and in memory of Louise

Contents

THREE

Introduction

I will not be able to gloss, cover, close-read, and celebrate all of the stellar poems in Jacob Eigen's *The Twenty-First Century*. There are too many. But the thinking—the thinking! (which is to say the feeling that takes place across this book)—is astounding. Just as I exit the final image or stanza of a poem, say "The End of the Long, Miserable Evening" for instance, I find myself plunging back into the poem immediately, moving backwards, wondering how did I, the reader, get here. How did I begin in a parking lot then suddenly meet an ibis that stands in a puddle that bears its reflection only for the ibis to become "two pigeons mounting each other and flapping / each one covering itself with the other?"

While Eigen might have a surrealist mind, he also announces a poesis, a poetics, that believes in the humility of revision as the generative engine of the poem. It's as if he turns to the poem and asks, "what next?" What might the poem have me discover about language, the soul, cruelty, power, loneliness? He trusts, or, more so, he believes in the materiality of language to reveal its ruptures, raptures, and limits. The ruptures, raptures, and limits of us, the ones who make and bear the marks of language, of living in language's cities and locked rooms.

So, he turns to language not because it releases him from the grime and banality of the world but precisely because it tethers him to it. Tethers him to its strangeness, to its fruitful and terrifying juxtapositions. In "The Longing in the Heart of the Vizier," Eigen occupies the mind and ear of a vizier who stands on a balcony taking in the sounds and images of a city below him. The poem feels as if it's moving toward rapture, when Eigen turns our attention to a "jangling noise," a noise that is "bright but far away." However, Eigen slowly dials up the complication of the noise, of this potential beauty when the vizier likens the sound to the "sultan's concubines shaking the silver on their ankles in one of the locked rooms," which we understand the vizier finds titillating and beautiful. However, as the reader, we understand that nothing in a locked room can be beautiful, especially not people. Eigen ratchets up the tension in the next sentence by revealing that when the vizier actually looked in the direction of the jangling, the noise was "the sound of the prisoners dragging their chains through the sand, on their way to the executions he himself had scheduled for the rising of the sun." In that moment, we understand that the city below the vizier's sight and mind, beneath his power, reflects his inability to make or bear beauty. That he, the vizier, has built of box of cruelty that he himself is locked into. What is also profound and deft about this moment is that we are reading a prose poem. Eigen is revealing to us—readers, writers, viziers (of sorts)—that we too make boxes and locked rooms of cruelty.

Eigen's use of and interrogation of form is also manifested in his uncanny use of framing and persona. For instance, in "October," Eigen writes again from the close-third person perspective of a spider, ruminating upon his life and his daily labors. However, this is no ordinary spider. Yes, it is going on its daily spiderly duties like "exuding" webs and trapping flies, but it also "considers its earlier life as a man who lived in Queens, New York." While this might seem hokey; it is not. Reminiscent of James Tate's "The Promotion," a poem in which a man reflects on his former life as a dog, Eigen's spider, who was once a man, remembers Queens life as that which was adrift, a life without mooring or purpose. Eigen writes:

Yes,

he told the fly as he bound it,
I remember lying in bed in Queens
And watching snow accumulated
on the windowsill, when I didn't know

what I was, or what to kill to be happy.

"What to kill to be happy." That phrase stuns me. I play it over and over in my mind. I'm in awe of it because it feels like that moment in Wallace Stevens "Rabbit as King of the Ghosts" when the rabbit becomes the great being, the large thing in the sky, an entity no longer subjected to the murderous desires of a cat. However, Eigen writes from the other side, from the position of the spider who feels more at peace, more in and of himself, because he knows what to kill to make him happy. I don't believe we are to uncritically accept the spider's happiness. However, we are to sit with spider's happiness, with its connection to its sustenance, its viability, which is to say, its life.

In another twist, Eigen complicates the situation of the bound fly passively listening to its predator. The fly, too, remembers its past life as a human in Queens. Unlike the spider who spent his human years searching for meaning, for mooring, the fly responds:

I too lived in Queens, but I never left

my apartment. Balancing
the take-out on your handlebars,

weaving your way through the slush—
what did you think you would find
out there?

In the fly's response, there's a defamiliarization of the familiar, of the notion that everything in the human life is moving teleologically toward some sort of apotheosis, some beautiful end. The fly knows this not to be true because he is there ensnarled in the web of the spider, that soon the toxins the spider secretes will dissolve its body "overnight."

I'm enthralled with Jacob Eigen's heart, his nimble mind, and the thinking—the thinking! (which is to say the feeling in these poems). I hope you will be too.

Roger Reeves
February, 2024

It's true, said the stalk of wheat
no one liked —

we will be cut from our mother and crushed.

ONE

The Difficult Years

We were roaches in those days retreating into the walls, dreaming our useless wings might finally transform and allow us to fly. Or we were fish inside a tank in Chinatown with our glossy eyes pressed against the algae. *Are we dead,* you would ask, and yet we were still talking. Or were we talking? A cleaver was beating a cutting board in a kitchen above us, like a round of applause. *They're cheering for us!* you would say. *But who are we...* I would ask. *Who are they...*

Soul

Crushed by its parents' union
it foams up and spills over
into the realm of substances.

What it needs it takes
by controlling muscles
or producing sounds.

Only the sensation of motion
reminds it that wherever
it had existed, it had existed

swaying, which is why
its parents put it to sleep
in the Saab, driving in circles.

◆ ◆ ◆

Not much is asked of it:
to feed, to grow. Naturally

it distinguishes between things
that are warm and moving and those
that are cold and still —

in no category can it place objects
like pinwheels, which move
without being touched.

⋄ ⋄ ⋄

Now it's a child. It doesn't know why
playing some video games makes it nervous.

A man falls through green rings,
a car jumps over missing
sections of an elevated highway.

It explodes
these surrogate bodies, an eerie music
gets stuck in its head. Then it goes

downstairs to eat granola bars
while its mother makes dinner.

⋄ ⋄ ⋄

The warm things are *living*,
the cold things are *dead*.
But what does this mean?

Its grandfather is dead: this much it knows
because it sits in a limo
and its cousin gives it a huge grey vitamin

when she has no candy
and doesn't know what else to do.

But what about the Xeroxes
its father sometimes gives it,
still warm from the green light?

◆ ◆ ◆

Everything exists twice: once
for the adults, once for the children, so that
it never knows if it lives
in the echo or the original sound.

It looks at its body in the mirror — this,
it thinks, will enter the adult world.

But it doesn't. Even in high school
it seems to be the same body, always the same.

◆ ◆ ◆

In college it argues about Plato: the idea
that the soul maintains an independent
existence, untouched
by life, like a jacket
left under the seat at a theater. It argues

with men, and also with a woman
who says more adamantly
that the body is *a thing, a thing.*

It argues because it disagrees, but also
because it likes hearing the woman say this.

◆ ◆ ◆

The woman vanishes.

It goes to the gym
and causes itself pain, kisses
breasts and necks in bed, chews
tobacco, lives according to its estimate of its needs

until it resolves this is not its life.
Then it lies in bed and hangs its head
over the edge of the mattress
like a bat.

◆ ◆ ◆

Here we are in the night,
it says to itself.

The room is dark. The air is cold.
The superintendent never fixed the window.

◆ ◆ ◆

It falls asleep and dreams of the shimmering
green sheer plastic grass
its parents stuffed into Easter baskets.

Was all of that really just plastic cellophane,
it asks itself. *Yes*, it answers,
and *no* —

◆ ◆ ◆

Like the argument about what to send
into space. Its friend said Shakespeare,
but it wanted to send slips of paper
from Chinese fortune cookies,

so that many years from now
the aliens might find something
that said *GOOD LUCK*
IS COMING YOUR WAY —

and the alien scientists, exhausted
in their plastic ships, breathing
the artificial air

might think *could it be*
they are right, these extinct humans?

◆ ◆ ◆

Nothing lasts: that's what it thinks.
But why does it think this

shaking its head, as if it were
telling a brilliant joke?

A Theory

Before the invention of the alphabet,
when our ancestors were still leaving their handprints
on the walls of their caves in red ochre,

many lacked fingers or half-fingers
and appear to have suffered from frostbite,
though some archaeologists believe
these missing digits were not the result of medical
intervention

but rather ritual amputation. Perhaps
the most likely explanation is that both are true:

seeing one unique print, the others understood
there was something to be envied
and began severing parts of themselves,
stenciling the walls not just with images of animals

and rivers, but also these weird symbols,
accidentally discovered, that seem to say
this one standing here now, me.

The Returning Guests

We now entered the next phase of the evening. Soon we would receive our seat assignments, someone would make a speech, dinner would be served. But in the meantime we waited, chatting in small circles as the air grew cold. The women, bare-shouldered, began to reach into their purses for scarves. And with less and less to say, we found ourselves listening to the sound of the sea: the distant waves pulling each other in, one after the other, in meaningless repetitions. And yet, we thought, the bubbles in our glasses are still rising. Why this was a contradiction, we weren't sure. But there they were, going up and up and up — as though what? And then we looked up as well, and the chairs were all gone, the tables too, and someone we'd never met was motioning us into a tent, saying *Come on, come right now, they've already started without you.*

The Procession

The umbrellas are all going home.
They are all going to become
their thin, dry selves.

Unity

1.

All the other soldiers rushed toward the man-eating plant
and were taken

into it. They became it: they were its flowers.
While the one who'd been blinded
in battle by an alien fungus was grabbed on the leg

by a snake, which wrapped itself around his body
and said, *I'll be your eyes.*

Then everyone was rescued in a remarkable feat of strength.
The possibility that a person could be consumed entirely
was immediately superseded by triumph,
as was the alternative of wandering blind and asphyxiated.

2.

Listening to the ice cream truck
in bed, when it still sings
on the street because, your parents say,
its song is connected to its motor, you wonder

why it keeps going when children
are supposed to be sleeping. Each time
the song repeats it sounds the same

but is not the same,
like the identical streetlights: the one

illuminating the yellow house
across the street, the other
shining through the window
onto the wooden frog puppet on your door.

3.

The song fades. The house
is silent, or almost silent:

your brother turns the metal knobs
in the bathroom, the crickets
crawl over each other
in the lizard's cage.

How old the puppet seems
in the dark room,
almost ancient —
his strings and his crown.

Above him,
glow-in-the-dark clusters of dots
signifying stars.

The Southern Hemisphere

They are out there somewhere,
the lovers at summer camp.

It's February here. That means
they must be on the other side of the equator.

Soon their counselors will arrive
in golf carts, shining flashlights
to herd them back to their bunks.

Therefore they take this time
to whisper nothings to each other.

Nothing, nothing, nothing, nothing,
nothing, they whisper

in Australian accents. *All of this*
will be nothing. A journal entry describing
the scent of grass in the dark.

TWO

The Longing in the Heart of the Vizier

As the vizier stood on his balcony and watched the domes surface from the darkness, he felt that sensation he had felt as a boy, hearing girls laugh at a distance — only now this sensation was more unfathomable, coming late in life, after experience had taught him that those girls, and he himself, were nothing but decorated pots of blood. A blue light shimmered across the finials with a strange but familiar glow. Had he seen it before at the quicksilver mine in Idrija, or on the pile of iridescent squid the ink merchant gutted at the Yarmouk bazaar? He squinted his eyes and listened. A group of birds rose all at once. A door opened. A whip somewhere stung a horse. And something else: a jangling noise beneath all this, bright but far away, as if the sultan's concubines were shaking the silver on their ankles in one of the locked rooms. But looking down, the vizier saw this was just the sound of the prisoners dragging their chains through the sand, on their way to the executions he himself had scheduled for the rising of the sun.

The Boy in the Jungle

1.

"Why don't you sing at the festival,"
the elders asked him. But he preferred
the swamp: the filth of it, the beetles
hatching from mounds of elephant dung,
the slugs copulating so slowly
they seemed to die on top of each other
as they sank into the rot of the leaves.
He waded in muck up to his calves
and sang. And as his voice echoed it became
deeper and deeper and farther and farther away.

2.

He loved the swamp as long as he was singing
inside it. But in the morning, scratching
his ankles and tonguing the grit in his teeth,
he had to admit it looked worse in the day.
The slugs that had clutched each other
armlessly in the dark had all disappeared —
only their cobwebby junk remained. The frogs
hummed on and on. And everything was just
what it was: flatulent mists rising from a planet
and toucans screeching as if they were drunk.

3.

At the festival, the elders poured honey wine
through the sockets of ancestral skulls
and everyone, even his own parents, danced
and traded partners in the totem's gaze —
while the singers (his brother among them)
sang the rain song, the war song, the song of the hunt.
"Someday you will understand these rituals,"
his mother said. But there was nothing here
of the swamp. Only the crocodile, skinned
and detoothed, spinning on a spit.

4.

"What should I do," he asked it as it revolved
and dripped streams of oil that sizzled up
from the open flame. "I want to sing,"
he said, "but I do not want to sing for victory,
fecundity, or slaughter." The crocodile
did not reply. And the slave cranking the spit,
whose only duty was to stand in the heat
to perform this single action for hours,
looked up from his work and asked,
"Why do you talk to something dead?"

5.

So the boy returned to the swamp
where the silence was louder than ever
and the waterbugs beat their wings
over the surface, searching always

for food. And again his voice echoed
and was transformed, returning in the tone
of one much older, so that he felt
as though this were the voice capable
of advising him, if only it could say
something other than what he said.

The Lab

The time after college is over. Everyone who went abroad has returned. We walk through Astoria in the evening and talk about our jobs. My friend interns in a lab and tells me about the monkey he observes. How do you know it's depressed, I ask. Because it behaves all the time the way it behaves when it's raining outside, he says. And there's only one monkey. If anything happens to it, the whole project's lost.

October

When he was a spider
exuding thread between rocks
he considered his earlier life as a man
and recalled with objective curiosity

the belief that pleasure, true pleasure,
constituted achievement. Yes,

he told the fly as he bound it,
I remember lying in bed in Queens
and watching snow accumulate
on the windowsill, when I didn't know

what I was, or what to kill to be happy.
I'd bike down Northern Boulevard

to the Thai place, thinking of the nights
I'd spent on a woman's couch:
the way we'd talk about nothing —
the Nigerian student in her middle school

or the watch I'd look at in the department store
while my mother tried things on.

That was your problem, said the fly
which looked fearless and elegant now,
no longer even beating its wings.
I too lived in Queens, but I never left

my apartment. Balancing
the takeout on your handlebars,

weaving your way through the slush —
what did you think you would find
out there? And with that
it extended its palpus to suck in

the toxins that would dissolve it
into bones and fluids overnight.

Norwalk

Children shrieking: some want to be
pushed on the swings and some don't.

A seagull takes the body of a baby
turtle from its shell
like a gray tongue, and shakes it
in tiny gestures with its neck,
no no no no. Is it possible

not to have a soul, or to have one
and think of it as an organ
made of paper and stained,

and to proceed? As in your dream
of a football team in formation,
running up ramps in a parking garage.

Light touches the surfaces. And the Russian man
in a red swimsuit holds his head
in the outdoor shower, like a child holding a globe.

Lessons in Physics

At the end of a game of miniature golf
your ball entered a pipe
that went somewhere you couldn't see
and made a saddish, being-swallowed sound.

◆

This could happen to anything
at any time, your brother explained:
a wormhole could come into existence
spontaneously and suck it in.

◆

Is this why some things
clung together so desperately?

Like the filaments of iron
your science teacher kept sealed in a Ziploc bag
because, she said, if they ever touched the magnet directly
they would never let it go.

◆

In an airless plastic bag tied with a knot
a few crickets always died
on the way back from the pet store
and the rest fed on their corpses.

Then you covered all of them with white
calcium powder, like room-temperature snow,

and dropped them into the lizard's tank
where they sang in the darkness.

◆

What would they sing?
Nothing. They just sang
themselves:
cricket, cricket, cricket...

The Destinationless Yacht

Wandering from the bridge to the bulwarks. Discussing the weather. Sitting in the evening room in the evening. Having a smoke. What else was there to do? Occasionally someone said *Let's organize a ball!* But these balls were always awful. Once the musicians learned how to seduce each other, they couldn't remember why they played music — their song became the sound of springs creaking, and this in turn became silence. *The problem*, the captain said, *was believing I was a captain simply because I liked wearing a hat with an anchor and a shining black brim.* And the bottles on the wall, shaking against each other, made the sound of rain falling into the ocean.

The Captain's Parrot

The parrot recalled those phrases the captain had taught it in its youth: *heave-ho-ahead* and *a-pirate's-life-for-me.* But when it uttered them now, the captain gave it a mournful look, or told it to shut up, or even flicked it painfully with a bootlace. When the parrot instead tried imitating what it heard from the captain more recently — the weeping, the sighs — he beat it even harder. But what else could it do? It could only sing what it heard. So it learned to imitate the ocean slapping the flank of the boat, the ice clinking in the captain's glass, and even the snap of the whip that hit it. That was how we found it: in a bad state, living in a cage filled with its own dried feces and shed feathers, with the sounds of the world inside it.

THREE

The Twenty-First Century

In those days, Japanese restaurants placed tanks of fake, magnetic fish
in their vestibules. We would sit at the counter saying I love so-and-so
but live with so-and-so-someone-else, and the waiter folding napkins
at the corner table would look up from his work and say: *please*
see the fish—the way they approach one side of the tank and then the
other,
turning and turning in a way that makes us feel they're alive.
But he would say this in Japanese, which at that time we heard
as a sequence of meaningless syllables. Because it would be many years
until the distinction between all languages was erased.
And for us, many bowls of clouded broth.

The Wind

1. *The Numerical Order*

From the snow, a shape is forming:
the outline of a man
as he walks away from Queens Boulevard
and the cabs in the evening.

He passes the glowing windows
at the gas station, the trash heaps.

Some things cannot be weighed,
he remembers Leibniz saying,
and some things cannot be measured,
but there is nothing which cannot be numbered.

This axiom applies to everything,
he thinks. Even him. One man in the snow.

2. *The Fish Sticks*

The fish sticks look especially dead tonight —

as though they were not
the reprocessed flesh of fish
but themselves used to swim
and have eyes.

They are dead
and so they have nothing to say
about the window rattling in the wind or
about being consumed.

Only the moon in the window
seems to say
and yet —

as in:

and yet here I am
moving through the dark.

3. *Bedtime*

Soon he too will be sleeping
and the world will continue without him.
The birds will eat wood
and the men in blue hats will come for the recycling.

One, two, three,
he counts to himself in the dark room —
sheep? Or something else we can't see?

The only other thing speaking
is the car alarm
set off by nothing
cycling through tones in the distance.

The End of the Long, Miserable Evening

We were walking through the Costco parking lot.
The wind was sighing through the buildings
and we had stopped speaking long ago.

It's not too late to admit that we really do lack a purpose,
you said. Like this ibis on the water, balancing on its reflection.
And there was an ibis, standing in one of the black puddles.

But as soon as we saw it, it transformed
into two pigeons mounting each other and flapping,
each one trying to cover itself with the other.

God

God walks at the time of the evening breeze. He prefers not to go out at noon when the sun reveals creation completely. Not bad, he says. Let the book attest that it was good and that I said that it was good. Particularly this sound, he continues off the record. Was that my genius, to separate these creatures from each other? Who knew that these geese, for instance, would make such a low, desperate sound?

Epithalamium

Think, however, of the moment
the scent of seaweed first enters
your rented car, reminding you
and the person next to you
it's alright to mate with each other —
other organisms do it,
other organisms even let themselves die
after years of clinging to shells
like little invisible white knuckles.
Enough music for now, you say.
And the road you know belongs
to the wind and the insects
seems, for those miles,
to belong to you, too.

The Cartographer's Blue Period

One day an old sailor asked to take a closer look at the big map behind the counter. *Drawn during the cartographer's blue period,* the shopkeeper said. *I didn't know cartographers had blue periods,* the sailor replied. Still he inspected it, moving his spectacles closer and farther from his eyes. It was very blue indeed. The lands and the oceans were all blue, as were the labels, which he could barely make out by squinting. *I like it,* he finally said, and he lay a stack of gold ducats on the table. The shopkeeper could hardly conceal his surprise. He had never understood why anyone would make a blue map, or why anyone else would buy one, or why he himself had left it hanging there so long. He was even tempted to ask why the sailor liked it, but as he removed the map from the wall he was distracted — there was a bright spot, an unfaded rectangle of wallpaper where the map had been. Everywhere else those curlicue birds had become vague outlines, bleached by the sun. But here, protected by the map all these years, they were still nesting with each other, aiming their beaks in flight. *That's it,* said the sailor, as if somehow he could tell what the shopkeeper was feeling. *That's what I've been searching for. You can't get any bluer than that.*

This Poem Will Self-Destruct

Therefore
it is your mission should you choose to accept it
to do what you are doing now:
to read it. Knowing that

if you fail, the same events will occur as if you succeed —
the same, but in a slightly
lonelier version, in which
we go back to sleep, never having met.

Ilyana

1.

Nothing is happening.
The mannequins in the window
of the used clothing store
look just as bored as you.

A livery cab idles by the curb.
A child removes a donut
from a paper bag and throws
the bag onto the street.

2.

Am I squandering the hours,
you say, becoming a character
in a Chekhov play? Of course
you are, a bald man says

from the window of the cab.
Like that paper bag — that's how
you're blown from one day
to the next, until you disappear.

3.

Now Ilyana steps from the cab,
straightening her patterned Russian
gloves that have no English name.
How long has it been, she asks.

Are you still writing poems
about your childhood? Do they
rhyme? Are they any good?
As for me, I'm the same,

4.

incapable of love, like a horse
who must be whipped
and even then won't move.
The child I was is dead,

you say. I am entirely a man.
I wake and sleep and sometimes
go to bars. Ah, Jacob Jacobovich,
she replies. Don't despair —

5.

there is a time, even if it is
very brief, between
the beginning and the end.
And she smiles as she sinks

back into the darkness
of the cab, extending her arm
with the wrist ideally bent
to receive a ceremonial kiss.

The Lost Tea Rooms of His Youth

To be bald, to sit under a light with no fixture, to smoke, to compose verses that rhymed in Russian and achieved a stark brilliance in translation: this was his goal. And yet he was not bald, he had no taste for cigarettes, and he spoke no Russian. Nevertheless, he sat under the fixtureless light, imagining the gold embroidery of the tablecloths, the generals flirting with the women. And in this way he began to feel that he was far from home even while he was at home.

Boethius' Body

A few years after the execution,
when it had completed its time as a corpse
and had transformed into moisture and rot,

the matter that had once composed the body
of Anicius Malius Severinus Boethius
was shoveled into a wheelbarrow
and moved to the crypt of a church. At least

this was true of the skeleton, while
probably the eyes
the soldiers squeezed from the head
had already deteriorated — along with the brain
that leaked out when they bludgeoned the body to death.

Take unity away from a thing and existence too
ceases, that brain
had once thought. And in the moment
it transmitted this thought to the muscles in the hand,

it must have believed it would go on living, just as
all of us believe we will go on living
when we say *I will die* but really mean
here I am, thinking. And silently,

it commanded its hand to transcribe those words
while the soldiers sat outside its cell,
playing cards and throwing
knuckles of animal bone down the long Roman table.

The Box of Toys

Severed arms, rubber bands,
heads, guns, legs, breastplates, birds:
the chest contained all these.
It seemed to contain even
what might no longer be in it,
what you remembered and lost.

The Thirteen Chambers of the Heart

The roaches will breed long after you are gone.
Breed and mutate.
Until on a dark evening
like this one, under a streetlight in the rain

one will stop on his way home
and rub his mandible with one of his six hands —
the sign (as always) that he has started composing a poem.

There is no end, he thinks. *It all goes on and on.*
And as he thinks, he weeps

from his eyes, his many eyes,
even the secret, vestigial ones
that always seemed so useless to him,
which his ancestors required in ancient times

because they were very small and lived
inside the walls. *The way we all live*

in the darkness of time, he goes on writing,
searching for a way to arrive at that idea
which has suddenly occurred to him —

to compare the hollows of those walls
to the thirteen chambers of the heart.

But then again perhaps
another organism will read his work someday,
one with a different physiognomy,

like those mysterious human beings
whose bones he used to see, as a child, in museums.

Summer

At 2:00 AM, he watches the fan
and holds a can of frozen lemonade

against his bites. Your voice,
he thinks, will cease
like that, like the bite that irritates
then disappears. *And yet*

that voice starts to say. And yet
what? And yet we are here?

Notes

Unity

The movie described in the first section is *GI Joe: The Movie,* the animated feature from 1987. When a team of Joes escapes from capture, they run into battle and are swallowed by a giant, man-eating plant. Only one, listening to the advice of Cobra Commander—his former nemesis— manages to break free. He is blinded in the process, however, and must rely on Cobra Commander's directions as the two of them wander out into the arctic wilderness.

The Wind

The Leibniz quotation comes from JL Austin's translation of *The Foundations of Arithmetic* by Gottlob Frege. The full text reads: "Some things cannot be weighed, as having no force and power; some things cannot be measured, by reason of having no parts; but there is nothing which cannot be numbered. Thus number is, as it were, a kind of metaphysical figure."

Boethius' Body

Boethius' quoted thought comes from Victor Watts' translation of *The Consolation of Philosophy*, the treatise Boethius wrote in prison while awaiting execution. In the third book, Lady Philosophy tells him: "whatever seeks to subsist and remain alive desires to be one; take unity away from a thing and existence too ceases."

Acknowledgements

These poems were written in the course of many trips to and from Cambridge, Berkeley, and Vermont, where Louise Glück patiently read them — before taking their author out to dinner to toast the triumph of having discovered a beginning, an ending, or even a single line. She isn't here to see the printed volume, but in a sense she was the first to read it.

Deep gratitude to Roger Reeves for hearing these lines — for really hearing them — and to Elizabeth Scanlon, for transforming them into a book with an ISBN, made of actual paper and glue.

Thank you to the editors of periodicals where some of these poems appeared: Meghan O'Rourke at *The Yale Review* ("The Twenty-First Century," "October," "Boethius' Body," and "The Southern Hemisphere"), Bob and Peg Boyers at *Salmagundi* ("Lessons in Physics"), and Evan James at *The Iowa Review* ("The Monkey," "The End of the Long, Miserable Evening," and "The Difficult Years"). Thanks also to those who sponsored unofficial residencies in their offices and homes, particularly Frank Raffaele, Abe King, and Gene Sky in Queens and Cathy Gruber in Chicago.

Thanks, always, to my parents, my brother, and Emma.

And thank you, too — whomever, wherever you are. You've read to the end. As they say in *Spaceballs*: if you can read this, you don't need glasses.